Lucky L

Contents

by
Margaret Ryan
illustrated by
Jacqueline East

Chapter 1

Football, Football, Football!

Dean loved football. He played every day at school. He played every day at home. He played every night in his sleep.

Dean had a little sister.

She was called Sarah.

Sarah loved football, too.

She played for a team

called 'The Pink Panthers'.

One day Sarah said, "Come and play football with me, Dean."

"No way!" said Dean. "Footballs are not pink. Anyway, I don't play football with girls."

"I can help you to get into the school team," said Sarah. "Then we will both be in a team."

"I don't need your help," said Dean.

"You will have to do well at the trial to get into the team," said Sarah. "I can help you. Please come and play with me."

"No, I have got things to do," said Dean.

Chapter 2

The Trial

It was the day of the trial. Dean put his football kit into his bag and set off.

Dean got to school. Sarah was there. "Good luck, Dean!" she shouted. Dean looked the other way.

Dean played his best football. A player kicked and pushed him but Dean played on.

Sarah saw the kicking and pushing. She shouted to the referee, "Send that bully off!"

Then the referee saw the kicking and pushing, too. He sent the bully off.

After the game, the teacher said, "You played a good game, Dean. You are in the team on Saturday against Hill Street School."

Dean was happy that he was in the team. Sarah was happy that he was in the team, too. She ran up to Dean and kissed him. "Stop that!" shouted Dean.

"You played a good game, Dean," said Sarah. "Did you see me get that bully sent off? I told you I could help you."

Chapter 3

The Big Game

The big day came at last. "Have my new pink laces for your boots," said Sarah. "Yours look a bit worn out."

"No way!" said Dean. "Pink is for girls."

"Can I come with you to the match?" said Sarah.

"No," said Dean. "I don't want you to come at all."

Dean set off for the match. He did not want Sarah to go with him. But she went anyway. She wanted to help Dean.

Dean got ready for the match. The teacher told them about his plan for the game.

"That is a good plan," said Dean. He put on his kit and his boots.

The old worn laces snapped in two.

"Help!" said Dean.

"You can't play if you can't find new laces, Dean," said the teacher. "You should take care of your kit if you want to be in the team."

Dean was fed up. He went outside.

Sarah was there. "What's up?" she said.

"I need new laces," said Dean. "My old laces snapped in two."

“Here,” said Sarah, “Have my laces.”

“No way!” said Dean. “Pink laces are for girls!”

“Pink laces or no game!” said Sarah.

“OK,” said Dean.

Dean played a good game. He scored two goals against Hill Street. He was the man of the match.

"You played a good game, Dean," said the teacher. "Your pink laces must be lucky!"

"Yes," said Dean. "Now I'm going to wear lucky pink laces for every game!"